I would like to dedicate this book to my grandchildren (Colin, Maya, Patrick, and Jaya) and to grandchildren everywhere. May we forever love and learn together.

Flowers from A to Z That We See

Flowers here.
Flowers there.
Flowers everywhere.

Flowers from seeds.
Flowers from bulbs or buds.
Flowers we want and flowers from weeds.

Flowers produce seeds.
Seeds that grow to be fruit on trees.
Seeds that grow to be the grains that we need.

Some flowers come back year after year.
Others don't return.
Save those seeds and plant again or they will disappear.

Flowers on the ground.
Flowers on bushes and trees.
Come see the flowers that we found.

Aa: <u>Azaleas</u> -
Look for us each spring when gentle rains fall.
Standing proudly along the wall.
In sun we grow rounded. In shade we grow tall.

African Marigolds

Apple Tree

Asters

B: Black-Eyed Susans -
Look for us each summer - yellow with oval leaves.
We are food for butterflies and bees;
Our seeds feed small birds like chickadees.

Begonias

BlueBells

Bleeding Heart

Blue Star

Buttercup

Blue Star Creeper

Barberton Daisies

Bloody Cranesbill

Blue Star Creeper

C: Clematis -
Look for us in spring and summer on vines old and new.
We come in many colors - purple, pink or blue.
Give us mulch and water or we will cry "Boo-hoo!"

Calliopsis

California Brittlebush

Cherry tree

Cinquefoil

Carnations

Cow Parsley

Columbine

Cosmos

D: Daisies -
Look for us in late summer or early fall.
Lovely green stems grow nice and tall.
White blossoms last with rain or none at all.

Dianthus - Sweet William

Dahlias

Daffodils

E: Echinaceas -
Look for us when summer leaves.
Blossoms can be made into teas.
Native to prairies without any trees.

Edging Lobelia

F: Forsythia -

Look for us early in spring as sprouts begin to grow.
Give us lots of sun or we will crouch down low.
Measure 6 feet between us as your seeds you sow.

Fuchsia

G: Geranium -

Look for us in spring and summer once the frost is past,
Deadhead us often so our blooms will last.
Bring inside when cold winds blow and we will everlast.

*Deadheading is removing spent blossoms…

Ground Ivy

Ground Elder

Glory of the Snow

Grape Hyacinths

H: Hydrangea -
Look for us in summer's warm.
Plant north or south of your house or dorm.
Look out for us in high winds and storms.

Hedgehog Cactus

Honeysuckle

Hyacinths

I: Iris -
Look for us late in spring, growing tall in the sun.
Plant us close to the surface when summer is done.
Watch us multiply as your garden we overrun.

Impatiens

J: Johnny Jump-ups -
Look for us in spring, down low.
Plant us once and watch us grow
As our seeds are blown.

K: Kalanchoes-
Look for us in hot climates or indoors.
Succulents, we hold water in our leaves.
Deadhead our blooms, we grow more.

L: Lilies of the Valley -
Look for us in woodlands come spring.
Short green stems and white blossoms.
Sweet smelling bells, can you hear us ring?

Lilac Bush

Lilly

Lobed Tickseed

M: Marigolds

Look for our bright orange blossoms in springtime.
Deadhead us so we will have a long lifetime.
We are a smelly plant yet rabbits like us at mealtime.

Magnolia

Mexican Bush

Mother of Thyme   **Mountain Laurel**

N: Narcissus -
Look for us as the snow melts dry.
Pollinators love us - bees and butterflies.
Underground we will divide and multiply.

O: Orchids -
Look for us in pots.
We like it nice and hot.
Cover our roots - Not!

P: Pansies -

Look for us in late spring sunshine
On little hills or pots that drain well.
We don't like hot, but cold is fine.

Periwinkle

Petunia

Peony

Phlox

Pink

Plantain Lily

Purple Leaf Plum

Pear Tree

Persian Buttercup

Poppy

Q: Quince -

Look for us to bloom in springtime.
You'll need two for fruit to grow.
Cooked as jelly it is sublime.

R: Rhododendrons -

Look for us in late spring after azaleas fade.
Plant us in full sun or partial shade.
Feed us coffee grounds, we've got it made.

Redbud

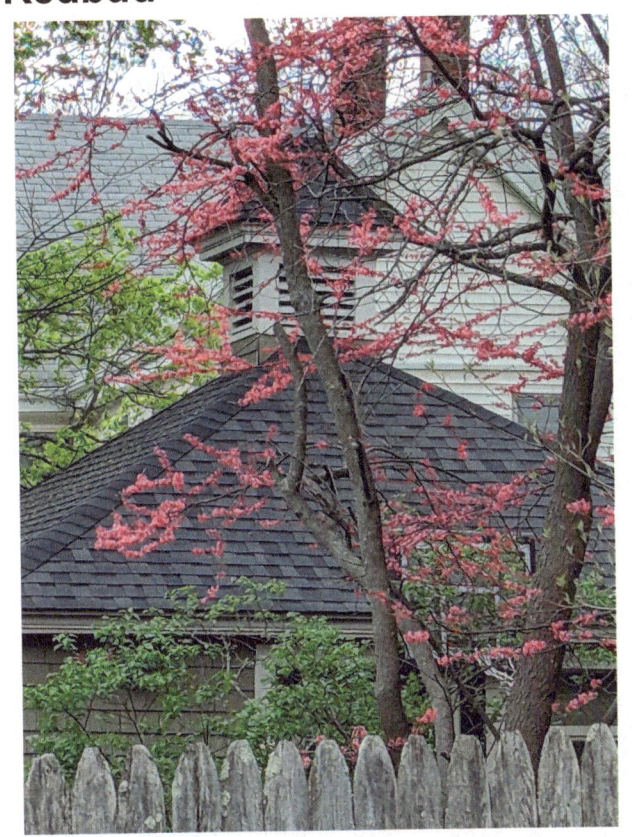

Red Powder Puff

Russian Sage

S: Sunflowers -

Look for us in summer or early fall.
Top-heavy, we need support to stand.
Hot summers, water us well so we grow tall.

Siberian Squill

Soap Aloe

Speedwell

Slender Yellow
Wood Sorrel

Spotted Nettle

Spurge (Cypress)

Squash blossoms

Strawberry bush

T: Tulips -
Look for us when winter's been put to bed.
We come in many colors - yellows, pinks, and reds.
Sprinkle cayenne pepper so bunnies don't eat our heads.

Tiger Lily

Trailing Ice Plant

U?
What begins with U?
Look for us in nurseries.
Find them? Tell me please.
Though some may be overseas…

Perennial flowers:
- **Uinta Basin hookless cactus - found in Utah**
- **Ulex - found in Africa and Europe**
- **Umbrella plant - found in California and Oregon**
- **Umbrella sedge - found in Africa and the Arabian Peninsula**
- **Upright clematis - found in Europe**
- **Urn plant - found in Brazil**
- **Uva-ursi - found in the mountains of Virginia, New Mexico, and California**

Annual Flowers:
- **Ursinia - found in South Africa**

V: Violets -

Look for us in spring - down low.
More and more each year we'll grow
In sunny spots that don't get too hot, you know.

W: Water Lilies -
Look for us in summer on slow-moving water.
Long stems from muddy bottoms anchor white blossoms.
Floating on creeks, rivers, ponds, or lakes if you prefer.

Windflowers

Woodland Phlox

X?
What begins with x?
Look for us in nurseries.
Find them? Tell me please.
Though some are overseas...

Annual Flowers:
- **Xanthisma - found in southwestern US.**
- **Xeranthemum - found in the Mediterranean and Asia**
- **Xerochrysum - found in Australia**

Perennial Flowers:
- **Xanthoceras - found in China**
- **Xerophyllum - found in British Columbia to California and east to the northern Rocky Mountains.**
- **Xylosma - found in Texas, Mexico, and Central America.**
- **Xyris - found in Cuba, and Texas to New Jersey.**

Y: Yellow Flag Iris -
Look for us at the end of May through July.
In 10 inches of water with muddy bottoms.
Watch us crowd out others as we multiply.

Yarrow

Z: Zinnia -

Look for us in summer and into the fall.
No need to transplant us.
Sowing seeds is a better protocol.

Dear Parents/ Teachers/ Guardians,
I hope you enjoyed this book. Maybe you'll begin noticing more flowers in your own neighborhood. Perhaps you want to know more about them. Great.

I tried to cover a lot of issues briefly. I mentioned a lot of things all flowers need - such as how much sun/ shade; water/ drainage; temperature range; fertilizer; space between plants; depth needed when planting; environment; propagation (process of increasing the number of plants); deadheading (removing spent blossoms); succulents (which store water in their leaves) vs. non-succulents; and whether it is best to transplant them or easier to start from seed. I have included both edible plants and ornamental plants.

I have included photos and descriptions of plants' physical characteristics such as color, size, leaves and stems.

I also tried to cover plants and their relationships to insects, birds, bunnies, and people. Along with this I have given a few hints on ways to protect plants from being eaten.

I have done all of this while trying to appeal to a younger audience by writing short stanzas that are fun to read aloud.

I hope you continue to share and learn about the world of flowers.

How I came to write this book….

I have taught since I was 6 years old, returning home each day from school to teach my 5 younger siblings.

Today you can be a teacher too with the power of technology.

I used an app called, "Picture This" and 'googled' to research the flowers I have chosen to write about. There are many great gardening websites including: cleanairgardening.com; gardeningknowhow.com; almanac.com; provenwinners.com; gardenerspath.com; and thepracticalplanner.com to name a few.

I hope you find joy in the beauty and wonder of flowers.

Made in the USA
Columbia, SC
26 July 2023